JAR
SALADS

JAR SALADS

52 HAPPY, healthy lunches

ALEXANDER HART

Smith
Street
Books

CONTENTS

JAR SALADS
introduction

There are so many benefits in bringing a homemade salad to work. It's healthy, low-cost, and it will taste better than any sad, over-priced sandwich from the shop down the road. The unfortunate reality, however, is that after being piled into a plastic container with a poorly fitting lid, by lunchtime that once-perky salad, so lovingly prepared, has usually turned into a depressingly soggy, limp mess.

Jar salads are the perfect solution to disappointing work lunches. They're portable and, above all, they will keep all of your ingredients fresh and crisp. Kept in the refrigerator, they store well enough that you can even make a week's worth of lunches in one go, so you're not spending every evening or early morning preparing your next midday meal.

With 52 recipes — one for every week of the year — including a whole chapter of vegetarian salads and many gluten-free options, *Jar Salads* has everything you need for happy, healthy lunches.

HOW DO JAR SALADS WORK?

The key to a successful jar salad is in the layering. Rather than mixing everything together, the dressing sits in the bottom of the jar, with the rest of the ingredients layered on top, from robust to delicate. The heavier, more resilient ingredients sit in and above the dressing, protecting the upper layers from going soggy. As long as the jar is kept upright, these ingredients will remain intact and at their best. Some vegetables such as cucumber, cauliflower, carrot and fennel will even improve their flavour over time, as the dressing will help to marinate or pickle ingredients that sit at the base of the jar.

WHAT KIND OF JAR SHOULD I USE?

The recipes in this book are designed for a 1 litre (1 quart/4 cup) jar. You can use any kind of glass jar as long as it has a tight-fitting lid. A jar with a wide mouth will make it easier both to assemble your salad and to shake it out when you want to eat it. A mason jar or similar is ideal.

WHY USE A GLASS JAR?

Aside from being the perfect shape for the layering technique described on the previous page, a glass jar allows for an airtight seal, ensuring freshness and avoiding salad-dressing spills in transportation. In addition, glass is food-safe and non-reactive, which is important when storing salad dressings due to their high acid content. Glass jars are perfect for the dishwasher, so they're much easier to clean when you're done.

WHERE DO I BUY JARS?

Mason jars are hugely popular and are readily available from kitchen supply, homeware and discount stores. Alternatively, there are plenty of online stores that stock jars in a variety of sizes for reasonable prices. Just remember to make sure you purchase jars with tight-fitting, preferably screw-top, lids.

WHAT ELSE DO I NEED?

A funnel is useful for pouring the dressing into the base of the jar, and a long-handled spoon and a pair of tongs are helpful for layering the ingredients.

HOW LONG WILL THE SALAD KEEP?

With a tightly sealed lid, jar salads can last for several days in the refrigerator – long enough to prepare a week's worth of lunches in advance. However, perishable ingredients such as seafood, meats, avocado, rice and egg should only be added the morning you plan to eat the salad, and should remain in the refrigerator until ready to serve.

HOW DO I EAT MY JAR SALAD?

Give the jar a bit of a shake with the lid still on to disperse the dressing, then open and tip the whole thing into a bowl. Give everything a mix and you're good to go.

HINTS AND TIPS

You can really use anything you want in your salad, just make sure you follow the layering method as described on the previous page. The recipes in this book should be used as a starting point and are simple to customise according to taste. The trick to a great jar salad is to ensure that it has a mix of textures, some kind of protein, something that's filling, and a good balance of flavours that include salty, sweet, bitter and acid.

Once you've tried a few different salads and developed a few favourites, it's great to have a few simple alterations in mind to keep things interesting. There's no need to eat the same lunch every day when there are so many simple ways to change things up. Variations might include the following:

Lettuce is not the only leaf out there. Mix up your greens. Kale, baby spinach and cabbage will give you a heartier, more substantial base; try some cress or snow pea shoots for something lighter and sweeter, or rocket (arugula), radicchio or witlof (Belgian endive/chicory) for a bitter, peppery taste. And don't be stingy with your soft fresh herbs – treat mint, coriander and basil as you would any other leafy green to give you an extra flavour hit.

Nuts and seeds offer a huge variety of flavours and textures, not to mention great nutritional benefits. A single salad can take on a whole new life just by changing or adding a source of crunch. Switch pine nuts for toasted pepitas (pumpkin seeds), use walnuts, pecans or hazelnuts instead of almonds, or add a spoonful of chia or linseeds (flax seeds) for extra protein. Just remember to keep nuts and seeds near the top layer of your jar salad so they stay perfectly crunchy.

Mix and match your dressings. The right dressing for the right salad is entirely up to personal taste. There are a variety of dressing recipes in this book, so get creative with your pairings. You can also easily create your own: a basic vinaigrette has a 3:1 ratio of oil to acid, which means there are endless permutations of oils (such as extra-virgin olive, avocado, peanut, sesame, grapeseed, walnut and linseed) and different acids (lemon, lime or orange juice and vinegars such as rice, apple cider, red wine, white wine, sherry and balsamic).

Add fresh or dried fruit. Whether it's the tang of a dried cranberry, the crisp bite of a slice of apple or the rich sweetness of mango, the right type of fruit can put a fresh and flavoursome spin on your salad. If you're adding fresh fruit such as apple or pear slices to a salad that you're preparing a few days in advance, first toss in some lemon or lime juice to stop the fruit from discolouring.

SHOPPING LIST

Constructing a jar salad doesn't need to be difficult — you can use ingredients you already have in your refrigerator or pantry. Basic ingredients to keep stocked for easy jar salad preparation include:

- extra-virgin olive oil
- citrus and vinegar (red wine, balsamic and rice vinegar; lemons, limes)
- mustard (dijon and seeded)
- leafy greens (mixed leaves, kale, baby spinach, rocket/arugula, cabbage)
- salad vegetables (tomato, cucumber, capsicum/bell pepper, carrot, corn, red onion, fennel)
- substantial vegetables (cauliflower, broccoli, pumpkin/winter squash, sweet potato, beetroot/beets)
- proteins (chickpeas, cannellini/lima beans, tofu, feta, tinned tuna, eggs, cooked chicken breast)
- grains and noodles/pasta (brown rice, quinoa, soba noodles, corn pasta, couscous)
- fresh herbs (coriander/cilantro, parsley, mint, basil)
- nuts and seeds (almonds, cashews, peanuts, pine nuts, pistachios, pepitas, sesame seeds, chia seeds)

Vegetarian

LEMONY ROASTED
CAULIFLOWER &
sugar—snap pea salad

MAKES
1

LEMON VINAIGRETTE

2 tablespoons extra-virgin olive oil
1½ tablespoons lemon juice
1 teaspoon lemon zest
½ teaspoon caster (superfine) sugar
½ teaspoon dijon mustard
salt & freshly ground black pepper

Mix together.

SUGAR-SNAP PEAS

100 g (3½ oz) sugar-snap peas

**Blanch in boiling water for 1 minute,
drop in ice water. Drain.**

ROASTED CAULIFLOWER

100 g (3½ oz) cauliflower,
cut into small florets

Mix in a bowl with:

¼ teaspoon minced garlic
1 teaspoon olive oil
1 teaspoon lemon juice
salt & freshly ground black pepper

**Once coated, tip onto a baking tray
and roast in 200°C (400°F) oven for
20–25 minutes, turning occasionally,
or until cooked. Allow to cool.**

OTHER INGREDIENTS

30 g (1 oz) toasted almonds,
roughly chopped
1 celery stalk, sliced
50 g (1¾ oz) red cabbage, finely shredded
handful of torn mint, to fill

MINT

ROASTED
CAULIFLOWER

RED CABBAGE

CELERY

SUGAR-SNAP PEAS

TOASTED ALMONDS

LEMON VINAIGRETTE

SWEET POTATO, FETA & SMOKED ALMOND *salad*

MAKES
1

RED-WINE VINAIGRETTE

2 tablespoons extra-virgin olive oil
1 tablespoon red-wine vinegar
½ teaspoon dijon mustard
salt & freshly ground black pepper

Mix together.

ROASTED SWEET POTATO

150 g (5½ oz) orange sweet potato,
cut into cubes

Mix in a bowl with:

1 teaspoon olive oil
salt & freshly ground black pepper

**Once coated, tip onto a baking tray
and roast in a 200°C (400°F) oven for
15 minutes, turning occasionally, or until
cooked. Allow to cool.**

OTHER INGREDIENTS

50 g (1¾ oz) feta, cut into cubes
30 g (1 oz) smoked almonds
handful of baby English spinach leaves, to fill

BABY SPINACH

SMOKED ALMONDS

FETA

ROASTED
SWEET POTATO

RED-WINE
VINAIGRETTE

SPICY
BUTTER BEAN SALAD

MAKES
1

LEMON & GARLIC DRESSING

2 tablespoons extra-virgin olive oil
juice of ½ lemon
1 teaspoon caster (superfine) sugar
¼ teaspoon minced garlic
salt & freshly ground black pepper

Mix together.

SPICY BUTTER BEANS

150 g (5½ oz) cooked butter beans
2 teaspoons olive oil
1 teaspoon ground cumin
½ teaspoon smoked paprika
¼ teaspoon cayenne pepper

Put all the ingredients in a plastic bag and shake until the butter beans are well coated. Heat in a frying pan until warmed through and fragrant. Allow to cool.

OTHER INGREDIENTS

1 zucchini (courgette), peeled into strips
¼ red onion, finely sliced
handful each of finely chopped
mint & basil leaves
handful of baby English spinach leaves, to fill

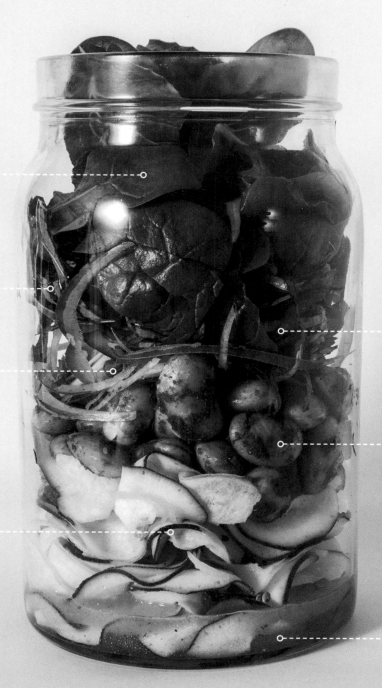

BABY SPINACH

BASIL

RED ONION

ZUCCHINI

MINT

SPICY
BUTTER BEANS

LEMON & GARLIC
DRESSING

LENTIL, BEETROOT & feta salad

MAKES
1

BALSAMIC VINAIGRETTE

2 tablespoons extra-virgin olive oil
1 tablespoon balsamic vinegar
1 teaspoon dijon mustard
salt and freshly ground black pepper

Mix together.

ROASTED BEETROOT

1 beetroot (beet), unpeeled

Cover in foil and roast in a 180°C (350°F) oven for 45 minutes, or until a skewer can be inserted into the flesh. Allow to cool, pull off the skin, cut into wedges.

OTHER INGREDIENTS

1 Lebanese (short) cucumber,
halved lengthways and sliced
150 g (5½ oz/⅔ cup) cooked brown lentils
30 g (1 oz) feta, crumbled
handful each of mint and baby English
spinach leaves, to fill

BABY SPINACH

MINT

ROASTED
BEETROOT

FETA

BROWN LENTILS

CUCUMBER

BALSAMIC
VINAIGRETTE

VEGGIE
TACO SALAD

MAKES
1

CORIANDER & LIME DRESSING

3 tablespoons Greek-style yoghurt
1 tablespoon apple cider vinegar
juice of 1 lime
large handful of coriander (cilantro),
finely chopped
pinch of caster (superfine) sugar
sea salt

Mix together.

OTHER INGREDIENTS

1 Lebanese (short) cucumber, diced
90 g (3 oz/½ cup) cooked black beans
2 tablespoons chopped jalapeños
1 tomato, diced
3 tablespoons corn kernels
½ avocado, sliced, with lemon juice
squeezed over
2 tablespoons shredded cheddar cheese
handful of chopped coriander (cilantro)
handful of baby English spinach leaves, to fill

BABY SPINACH

CORIANDER

CHEDDAR CHEESE

AVOCADO

CORN KERNELS

TOMATO

JALAPEÑOS

BLACK BEANS

CUCUMBER

CORIANDER &
LIME DRESSING

VEGETARIAN

CAPRESE PASTA SALAD

MAKES
1

PESTO DRESSING

2 tablespoons extra-virgin olive oil
2 tablespoons lemon juice
2 tablespoons pine nuts
large handful of basil
¼ teaspoon minced garlic
salt and freshly ground black pepper

**Whiz together in a food processor or pound
to a paste in a mortar with a pestle.**

OTHER INGREDIENTS

50 g (1¾ oz) fresh mozzarella,
cut into bite-sized pieces
100 g (3½ oz) cherry tomatoes, halved
60 g (2 oz) corn spiral pasta, cooked
handful each of torn basil & rocket
(arugula), to fill

ROCKET

BASIL

PASTA

CHERRY TOMATO

FRESH MOZZARELLA

PESTO DRESSING

CHARRED CORN & BEAN SALAD with lime VINAIGRETTE

MAKES
1

LIME VINAIGRETTE

2 tablespoons extra-virgin olive oil
1 tablespoon lime juice
salt & freshly ground black pepper

Mix together.

CHARRED CORN

1 ear of corn, husk removed
olive oil, to coat

Rub the corn with the oil. Grill on a char-grill pan over medium–high heat. Grill for 10–12 minutes, or until charred and cooked through. Remove, allow to cool, and cut the kernels from the cob.

OTHER INGREDIENTS

100 g (3½ oz) cherry tomatoes, quartered
100 g (3½ oz) cooked cannellini (lima) beans
2 spring onions (scallions), sliced
1 tablespoon grated parmesan
handful of torn basil leaves
handful of mixed salad greens, to fill

MIXED
SALAD GREENS

BASIL

PARMESAN CHEESE

SPRING ONION

CHARRED CORN

CANNELLINI BEANS

CHERRY TOMATO

LIME
VINAIGRETTE

HOKKIEN NOODLE SALAD

MAKES
1

SESAME-CHILLI DRESSING

½ teaspoon sesame oil
2 teaspoons rice vinegar
2 teaspoons light soy sauce
1 red chilli, seeded, finely chopped
2 teaspoons toasted sesame seeds
1 teaspoon caster (superfine) sugar

Mix together.

OTHER INGREDIENTS

1 carrot, spiralised
100 g (3½ oz) cooked hokkien noodles
2 spring onions (scallions), thinly sliced
50 g (1¾ oz) snow peas (mangetout),
thinly sliced
handful of bean sprouts
handful or coriander (cilantro), to fill

CORIANDER

BEAN SPROUTS

SNOW PEA

SPRING ONION

HOKKIEN NOODLES

CARROT

SESAME-CHILLI
DRESSING

LENTIL &
HALOUMI SALAD

MAKES
1

LEMON & CUMIN DRESSING

2 tablespoons extra-virgin olive oil
1½ tablespoons lemon juice
1 teaspoon ground cumin
salt & freshly ground black pepper

Mix together.

GRILLED HALOUMI

50 g (1¾ oz) slice of haloumi
2 teaspoons olive oil

Heat the oil in a frying pan over medium–high heat, add the haloumi and cook for 3 minutes on each side, or until browned. Allow to cool, cut into cubes.

OTHER INGREDIENTS

1 Lebanese (short) cucumber, diced
1 tomato, diced
150 g (5½ oz/⅔ cup) cooked brown lentils
2 tablespoons currants
handful each of mint & parsley, to fill

PARSLEY

MINT

CURRANTS

BROWN LENTILS

HALOUMI

TOMATO

CUCUMBER

LEMON & CUMIN
DRESSING

BROCCOLI, CARROT & CRANBERRY SALAD WITH *buttermilk dressing*

MAKES
1

BUTTERMILK DRESSING

3 tablespoons buttermilk
juice of ½ lemon
1 tablespoon snipped chives
¼ teaspoon minced garlic
salt & freshly ground black pepper

Mix together.

OTHER INGREDIENTS

100 g (3½ oz) small broccoli florets
1 small carrot, cut into matchsticks
¼ red capsicum (bell pepper), diced
¼ red onion, thinly sliced
3 tablespoons slivered almonds
2 tablespoons dried cranberries
handful of rocket (arugula), to fill

ROCKET

DRIED
CRANBERRIES

ALMONDS

RED ONION

RED CAPSICUM

CARROT

BROCCOLI

BUTTERMILK
DRESSING

QUINOA, ZUCCHINI
& *pea salad* WITH LEMON
& THYME DRESSING

MAKES
1

LEMON & THYME DRESSING

1½ tablespoons extra-virgin olive oil
1½ tablespoons lemon juice
1 teaspoon honey
1 teaspoon thyme leaves

Mix together.

QUINOA

65 g (2¼ oz/⅓ cup) quinoa

Put quinoa in a saucepan with 170 ml (5½ fl oz/⅔ cup) cold water. Cover, bring to the boil, then reduce the heat to low and simmer for 10–12 minutes, or until water is absorbed.

OTHER INGREDIENTS

1 zucchini (courgette), peeled into strips
50 g (1¾ oz/⅓ cup) cooked peas
30 g (1 oz) toasted almonds,
roughly chopped
handful each of mint & parsley, to fill

PARSLEY

MINT

TOASTED ALMONDS

QUINOA

PEAS

ZUCCHINI

LEMON & THYME
DRESSING

EDAMAME
& SOBA NOODLE SALAD

MAKES
1

SESAME & GINGER DRESSING

½ teaspoon sesame oil
1 tablespoon rice vinegar
1 tablespoon tamari or soy sauce
1 teaspoon finely grated ginger
1 tablespoon black sesame seeds

Mix together.

EDAMAME

200 g (7 oz) frozen edamame in shells

Blanch in boiling water for 3 minutes, drop in ice water. Drain and shell.

OTHER INGREDIENTS

1 Lebanese (short) cucumber, diced
120 g (4½ oz) cooked soba noodles
3 spring onions (scallions), finely sliced

SPRING ONION

EDAMAME

SOBA NOODLES

CUCUMBER

SESAME & GINGER
DRESSING

ROAST EGGPLANT, CHICKPEA & HERB SALAD
with lemon & SUMAC DRESSING

MAKES
1

LEMON & SUMAC DRESSING

2 tablespoons extra-virgin olive oil
2 tablespoons lemon juice
1 teaspoon sumac
½ teaspoon sweet paprika
¼ teaspoon minced garlic
½ teaspoon salt

Mix together.

ROASTED EGGPLANT

1 eggplant (aubergine), cut into
2.5 cm (1 inch) cubes

Mix in a bowl with:

1 tablespoon olive oil
salt & freshly ground black pepper

**Once coated, tip onto a baking tray
and roast in a 220°C (430°F) oven for
15 minutes, turning occasionally, or until
cooked. Allow to cool.**

OTHER INGREDIENTS

100 g (3½ oz) cooked chickpeas
¼ red capsicum (bell pepper), sliced
¼ red onion, thinly sliced
handful each of roughly chopped parsley
& mint, to fill

MINT

PARSLEY

RED ONION

ROASTED EGGPLANT

RED CAPSICUM

CHICKPEAS

LEMON & SUMAC
DRESSING

VEGETARIAN

BROWN RICE, BROAD BEAN & pomegranate salad

MAKES
1

POMEGRANATE MOLASSES DRESSING

2 tablespoons extra-virgin olive oil
juice of ½ lemon
2 teaspoons pomegranate molasses

BROAD BEANS

125 g (4½ oz) frozen broad (fava) beans

Blanch in boiling water for 3 minutes, drop in ice water. Drain and remove skins.

OTHER INGREDIENTS

½ small fennel bulb, finely sliced
with a mandoline
100 g (3½ oz/½ cup) cooked brown rice
¼ red onion, finely sliced
seeds of ½ pomegranate
handful of parsley, to fill

PARSLEY

POMEGRANATE
SEEDS

RED ONION

BROWN RICE

BROAD BEANS

FENNEL

POMEGRANATE
MOLASSES DRESSING

CARROT, ROASTED
CAPSICUM *& cashew salad*
WITH SESAME-CHILLI DRESSING

MAKES
1

SESAME-CHILLI DRESSING

½ teaspoon sesame oil
3 teaspoons rice vinegar
3 teaspoons light soy sauce
½ red chilli, seeded & finely chopped
2 teaspoons toasted sesame seeds
1 teaspoon caster (superfine) sugar

Mix together.

ROASTED CAPSICUM

1 red capsicum (bell pepper)

**Roast in a 200°C (400°F) oven for
15–20 minutes, turning occasionally,
until the skin is charred and blistered.
Transfer to a sealable plastic bag and set
aside for 10 minutes to steam. Peel the skin
and discard. Remove and discard the stem
and seeds. Thickly slice.**

OTHER INGREDIENTS

1 carrot, cut into matchsticks
30 g (1 oz) dry-roasted cashews
handful of baby English spinach leaves, to fill

BABY ENGLISH
SPINACH LEAVES

DRY-ROASTED
CASHEWS

ROASTED
CAPSICUM

CARROT

SESAME-CHILLI
DRESSING

ROASTED SPICED CHICKPEA & SWEET POTATO SALAD
with orange vinaigrette

MAKES
1

ORANGE VINAIGRETTE

2 tablespoons extra-virgin olive oil
1 tablespoon fresh orange juice
½ teaspoon dijon mustard
salt & freshly ground black pepper

Mix together.

ROASTED SPICED CHICKPEAS

150 g (5½ oz) tinned chickpeas

Mix in a bowl with:

1 tablespoon olive oil
juice of ½ lemon
1 tablespoon tamari or soy sauce
1 teaspoon honey
½ teaspoon ground cinnamon
½ teaspoon ground coriander
½ teaspoon ground cumin
freshly ground black pepper

Marinate the chickpeas for 20–30 minutes. Drain the marinade and spread the chickpeas in a single layer on an oven tray. Roast in a 200°C (400°F) oven for 30 minutes, or until lightly browned. Remove and allow to cool.

ROASTED SWEET POTATO

150 g (5½ oz) orange sweet potato, cut into cubes

Mix in a bowl with:

1 teaspoon olive oil
salt & freshly ground black pepper

Once coated, tip onto a baking tray and roast in a 200°C (400°F) oven for 15 minutes, turning occasionally, or until cooked. Allow to cool.

OTHER INGREDIENTS

30 g feta, cut into cubes
3 tablespoons slivered almonds
handful of rocket (arugula), to fill

ROCKET

ALMONDS

ROASTED SPICED
CHICKPEAS

FETA

ROASTED
SWEET POTATO

ORANGE
VINAIGRETTE

MARINATED TOFU SALAD
with spicy THAI DRESSING

MAKES
1

THAI DRESSING

½ teaspoon sesame oil
3 teaspoons lime juice
3 teaspoons fish sauce
½ red chilli, finely chopped
2 teaspoons caster (superfine) sugar

Mix together to dissolve the sugar.

OTHER INGREDIENTS

150 g (5½ oz) grape tomatoes, halved
1 Lebanese (short) cucumber, diced
3 tablespoons roughly chopped
roasted peanuts
handful each of roughly chopped coriander
(cilantro) & mint
handful of butter lettuce, to fill

MARINATED TOFU

150 g (5½ oz) firm tofu

First press out the excess liquid. Place tofu
between two paper towels on a plate. Place
a plate on top with a book or heavy weight
to push it down. Leave for at least
15 minutes. Cut into 2 cm (¾ inch) cubes.
Mix in a bowl with:

1½ tablespoons fish sauce
1 tablespoon rice vinegar
1 tablespoon lime juice
2 teaspoons caster (superfine) sugar
2 teaspoons chilli paste
1 teaspoon finely grated ginger

**Marinate for at least 1 hour. Drain the
marinade and bake in a 180°C (350°F) oven
for 20 minutes, turning halfway through
cooking, or until the tofu is golden brown.
Allow to cool.**

BUTTER LETTUCE

MINT

CORIANDER

ROASTED PEANUTS

MARINATED TOFU

CUCUMBER

GRAPE TOMATO

THAI DRESSING

MOROCCAN COUSCOUS, ROAST PUMPKIN & PRESERVED LEMON SALAD

MAKES
1

PRESERVED LEMON DRESSING

2 tablespoons extra-virgin olive oil
1 tablespoon lemon juice
1 preserved lemon quarter,
pulp discarded, peel finely chopped
salt & freshly ground black pepper

Mix together.

MOROCCAN COUSCOUS

125 ml (4 fl oz/½ cup) vegetable stock
95 g (3¼ oz/½ cup) instant couscous
1 teaspoon ground coriander
1 teaspoon ground cumin
1 teaspoon olive oil

**Bring the stock to the boil. Put the
couscous in a heatproof bowl or saucepan
with the coriander and cumin, stir through
the boiling stock. Cover and leave for
5 minutes. Top with the oil and fork
through the mixture.**

ROASTED SPICED PUMPKIN

100 g (3½ oz) pumpkin (winter squash),
cut into 2 cm (¾ inch) pieces

Mix in a bowl with:

1 teaspoon olive oil
½ teaspoon cinnamon
salt & freshly ground black pepper

**Once coated, tip onto a baking tray
and roast in a 180°C (350°F) oven for
15 minutes, turning occasionally, or until
cooked. Allow to cool.**

OTHER INGREDIENTS

10 pitted kalamata olives, chopped
2 tablespoons pine nuts
handful of parsley

PARSLEY

PINE NUTS

MOROCCAN COUSCOUS

ROASTED SPICED
PUMPKIN

KALAMATA
OLIVES

PRESERVED
LEMON DRESSING

TROPICAL *fruit salad* WITH MINT SYRUP

MAKES
1

MINT SYRUP

1 tablespoon caster (superfine) sugar
2 tablespoons warm water
5 mint leaves

Dissolve the sugar in the water in a small saucepan over low heat, add the mint leaves and simmer for about 5–10 minutes, until thickened. Discard the mint and allow to cool.

OTHER INGREDIENTS

100 g (3½ oz) fresh pineapple, cut into cubes
1 mango, cut into cubes
shaved fresh coconut from 1 young coconut
handful of mint

MINT

FRESH COCONUT

MANGO

PINEAPPLE

MINT SYRUP

THREE-BEAN salad

MAKES
1

LEMON VINAIGRETTE

2 tablespoons extra-virgin olive oil
1½ tablespoons lemon juice
1 teaspoon lemon zest
½ teaspoon dijon mustard
½ teaspoon caster (superfine) sugar
salt & freshly ground black pepper

Mix together.

BLANCHED EDAMAME

200 g (7 oz) frozen edamame in shells

**Blanch in boiling water for 5 minutes.
Allow to cool, then shell.**

OTHER INGREDIENTS

1 Lebanese (short) cucumber, diced
1 tomato, diced
50 g (1¾ oz) feta, cut into cubes
100 g (3½ oz) cooked black beans
100 g (3½ oz) cooked cannellini (lima) beans
handful of parsley

PARSLEY

EDAMAME

CANNELLINI BEANS

BLACK BEANS

FETA

TOMATO

CUCUMBER

LEMON
VINAIGRETTE

ROASTED BEETROOT
& pumpkin WITH QUINOA SALAD

MAKES
1

PRESERVED LEMON DRESSING

2 tablespoons extra-virgin olive oil
1 tablespoons lemon juice
1 preserved lemon quarter, pulp discarded,
peel finely chopped
salt & freshly ground black pepper

Mix together

ROASTED PUMPKIN

100 g (3½ oz) pumpkin (winter squash),
cut into 2 cm (¾ inch) pieces

Mix in a bowl with:

1 teaspoon olive oil
salt & freshly ground black pepper

**Once coated, tip onto a baking tray and
roast in a 180°C (350°F) oven for 15 minutes,
turning occasionally, or until cooked.
Allow to cool.**

ROASTED BEETROOT

1 beetroot (beet), unpeeled

**Cover in foil and roast in a 180°C (350°F)
oven for 45 minutes, or until a skewer
can be inserted into the flesh. Allow
to cool, pull off the skin, cut into
2 cm (¾ inch) pieces.**

QUINOA

100 g (3½ oz/½ cup) quinoa

**Put quinoa in a saucepan with 250 ml
(8½ fl oz/1 cup) cold water. Cover, bring
to the boil, then reduce the heat to low
and simmer for 10–12 minutes,
or until water is absorbed.**

OTHER INGREDIENTS

2 tablespoons pistachios
handful of baby kale leaves, to fill

BABY KALE

PISTACHIOS

QUINOA

ROASTED
BEETROOT

ROASTED
PUMPKIN

PRESERVED
LEMON DRESSING

VEGETARIAN

KALE &
TEMPEH SALAD WITH
tahini-miso dressing

MAKES
1

TAHINI-MISO DRESSING

½ teaspoon sesame oil
1 tablespoon rice vinegar
juice of ½ lemon
3 tablespoons tahini
3 teaspoons white miso
1 tablespoon water, to thin the dressing,
if necessary

Mix together.

OTHER INGREDIENTS

1 carrot, spiralised
100 g (3½ oz) ready-to-eat tempeh,
cut into cubes
1 tablespoon black sesame seeds
handful of baby kale leaves, to fill

BABY KALE

BLACK
SESAME SEEDS

TEMPEH

CARROT

TAHINI-MISO
DRESSING

SPICED LENTIL SALAD

LEMON DRESSING

2 tablespoons extra-virgin olive oil
1½ tablespoons lemon juice
salt and freshly ground black pepper

Mix together.

OTHER INGREDIENTS

½ red capsicum (bell pepper), diced
30 g (1 oz) hazelnuts, roughly chopped
2 tablespoons currants
1 tablespoon chopped capers
handful of roughly chopped mint
handful of rocket (arugula), to fill

SPICED LENTILS

2 teaspoons ground cumin
2 teaspoons ground coriander
1 teaspoon dried chilli flakes
150 g (5½ oz/⅔ cup) cooked brown lentils

Dry-fry the spices in a pan over medium heat until fragrant, remove from the heat and mix through the lentils.

ROCKET

MINT

CAPERS

CURRANTS

HAZELNUTS

SPICED LENTILS

RED CAPSICUM

LEMON DRESSING

FENNEL
& BROAD BEAN SALAD

MAKES
1

PRESERVED LEMON DRESSING

3 tablespoons white vinegar
1½ tablespoons lemon juice
1 preserved lemon quarter, pulp discarded,
peel finely chopped
3 teaspoons caster (superfine) sugar

Mix together.

BROAD BEANS

125 g (4½ oz) frozen broad (fava) beans

**Blanch in boiling water for 3 minutes, drop
in ice water. Drain and remove skins.**

OTHER INGREDIENTS

½ small fennel bulb, finely sliced
with a mandoline
50 g (1¾ oz) shredded red cabbage
handful of chopped mint
30 g (1 oz) grated parmesan
handful of mixed salad leaves, to fill

MIXED
SALAD LEAVES

PARMESAN

MINT

RED CABBAGE

BROAD BEANS

FENNEL

PRESERVED
LEMON DRESSING

SUMMER FRUIT SALAD WITH LIME YOGHURT & mint

MAKES
1

LIME YOGHURT

3 tablespoons Greek-style yoghurt
1 tablespoon lime juice
1 teaspoon caster (superfine) sugar
finely grated zest of 1 lime

Stir the sugar into the lime juice until dissolved. Combine with the yoghurt and zest.

OTHER INGREDIENTS

1 peach, cut into bite-sized pieces
125 g (4½ oz) blueberries
100 g (3½ oz) strawberries, cut into quarters
2 tablespoons slivered almonds
handful of mint

MINT

ALMONDS

STRAWBERRY

BLUEBERRIES

PEACH

LIME YOGHURT

SEAFOOD

CAJUN
PRAWN SALAD

MAKES
1

CAJUN SEASONING

1 teaspoon cumin seeds
1 teaspoon coriander seeds
1 teaspoon fennel seeds
1 teaspoon sweet paprika
1 teaspoon mustard powder
1 teaspoon ground oregano
½ teaspoon onion powder
¼ teaspoon garlic powder
¼ teaspoon cayenne pepper
½ teaspoon salt

Heat the cumin, coriander and fennel seeds
in a frying pan over low heat for 2 minutes,
stirring, until the seeds pop and the mixture
is fragrant. Remove to a mortar and pound
with a pestle to make a powder. Mix with
the remaining ingredients.

CAJUN PRAWNS

150 g (5½ oz) peeled and deveined
prawns (shrimp)
Cajun seasoning (recipe on left)
olive oil, for stir-frying

Toss the prawns in the Cajun seasoning
until well coated. Heat the oil in a frying
pan over medium–high heat and stir-fry
the prawns for about 3 minutes on
each side, or until cooked through.
Transfer to a bowl and allow to cool.

OTHER INGREDIENTS

juice of 1 lime
½ avocado, diced
¼ red capsicum (bell pepper), diced
handful of butter lettuce leaves, to fill

BUTTER LETTUCE

RED CAPSICUM

CAJUN PRAWNS

AVOCADO

LIME JUICE

NIÇOISE SALAD

MAKES
1

LEMON, ANCHOVY & CAPER VINAIGRETTE

2 tablespoons extra-virgin olive oil
2 tablespoons lemon juice
½ teaspoon dijon mustard
1 anchovy fillet, finely chopped
1 tablespoon capers, chopped
salt & freshly ground black pepper

Mix together.

OTHER INGREDIENTS

95 g (3¼ oz) tinned tuna, drained
100 g (3½ oz) cherry tomatoes, quartered
30 g (1 oz) black olives, sliced
1 hard-boiled egg, cut into quarters
handful of cos (romaine) lettuce,
cut into bite-sized pieces, to fill

COS LETTUCE

BLACK OLIVES

CHERRY TOMATO

TUNA

HARD-BOILED EGG

LEMON, ANCHOVY &
CAPER VINAIGRETTE

BARBECUED VIETNAMESE SQUID
& herb salad

MAKES
1

LEMON DRESSING

3 tablespoons lemon juice
1 teaspoon salt
½ teaspoons white pepper

BARBECUED SQUID

2 cleaned squid hoods, scored and sliced
1½ tablespoons olive oil
1 small garlic clove, crushed
1 small red chilli, seeded, finely chopped
1 lemongrass stem, white part only,
thinly sliced
1 red Asian shallot, cut in half, thinly sliced

OTHER INGREDIENTS

handful each of roughly chopped coriander
(cilantro) & mint
handful of rocket (arugula), to fill

Toss the squid in the oil and garlic.
Cook on a char-grill pan over high heat
for 2–3 minutes, turning, until curled
and golden. Remove from the heat, toss
through the chilli, lemongrass and shallot.
Set aside to cool.

ROCKET

MINT

CORIANDER

BARBECUED SQUID

LEMON DRESSING

TUNA, CANNELLINI BEANS, goji & kale salad

MAKES
1

CIDER VINEGAR DRESSING

2 tablespoons extra-virgin olive oil
1½ tablespoons apple-cider vinegar
½ teaspoon dijon mustard
½ teaspoon honey
salt & freshly ground black pepper

Mix together.

OTHER INGREDIENTS

100 g (3½ oz) cooked cannellini
(lima) beans
95 g (3¼ oz) tinned tuna, drained
3 tablespoons goji berries
30 g (1 oz) grated parmesan
handful of baby kale, to fill

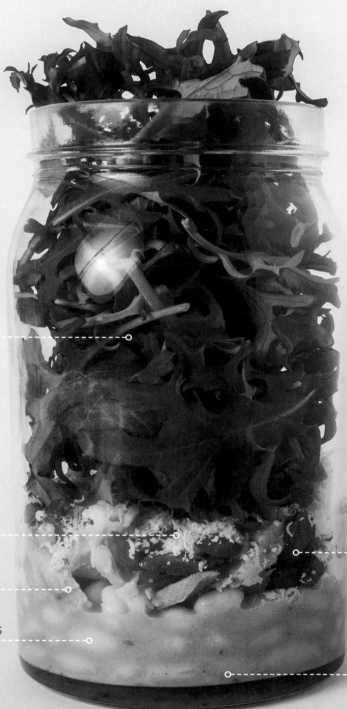

BABY KALE

PARMESAN CHEESE

GOJI BERRIES

TUNA

CANNELLINI BEANS

CIDER VINEGAR
DRESSING

CALIFORNIA ROLL SALAD

MAKES
1

CALIFORNIA ROLL DRESSING

1½ tablespoons whole-egg mayonnaise
1 teaspoon rice vinegar
1 teaspoon soy sauce
½ teaspoon wasabi paste

Mix together.

SEASONED CRAB

140 g (5 oz) crabmeat, cut into chunks
California roll dressing (recipe on left)

Mix together.

OTHER INGREDIENTS

1 Lebanese (short) cucumber, diced
100 g (3½ oz/½ cup) cooked brown rice
½ avocado, diced, with lemon juice
squeezed over
1 sheet nori, thinly sliced
handful of cos (romaine) lettuce,
cut into bite-sized pieces, to fill

COS LETTUCE

NORI

AVOCADO

BROWN RICE

CUCUMBER

SEASONED CRAB

PRAWN
cocktail salad

MAKES
1

COCKTAIL DRESSING

1 tablespoon whole-egg mayonnaise
2 teaspoons Greek-style yoghurt
2 teaspoons lemon juice
1 teaspoon tomato ketchup
½ teaspoon Worcestershire sauce
dash of Tabasco sauce
salt & freshly ground black pepper

Mix together.

COCKTAIL PRAWNS

150 g (5½ oz) cooked small
prawns (shrimp)
Cocktail dressing (recipe on left)
handful of roughly chopped mint

Mix together.

OTHER INGREDIENTS

½ avocado, diced, with lemon juice
squeezed over
150 g (5½ oz) cherry tomatoes, quartered
handful of shredded iceberg lettuce, to fill

ICEBERG LETTUCE

CHERRY TOMATO

AVOCADO

COCKTAIL PRAWNS

SMOKED SALMON, AVOCADO & ROCKET SALAD

MAKES
1

LIME & SESAME DRESSING

2 tablespoons extra-virgin olive oil
1 tablespoon lime juice
1 tablespoon toasted sesame seeds
salt & freshly ground black pepper

Mix together.

OTHER INGREDIENTS

1 Lebanese (short) cucumber,
cubed
100 g (3½ oz) smoked salmon slices,
cut into large bite-sized pieces
½ avocado, diced, with lemon juice
squeezed over
handful of rocket (arugula), to fill

ROCKET

AVOCADO

SMOKED SALMON

CUCUMBER

LIME & SESAME
DRESSING

POULTRY

JAPANESE
SESAME CHICKEN
& SOBA NOODLE SALAD

MAKES
1

CREAMY SESAME DRESSING

2 tablespoons whole-egg mayonnaise
2 teaspoons rice vinegar
1 teaspoon tamari or soy sauce
1 tablespoon tahini
½ teaspoon caster (superfine) sugar
pinch of salt

BLANCHED EDAMAME

200 g (7 oz) frozen edamame in shells

**Blanch in boiling water for 5 minutes.
Allow to cool, then shell.**

OTHER INGREDIENTS

1 carrot, cut into matchsticks
100 g (3½ oz) barbecued chicken, shredded
80 g (2¾ oz) cooked soba noodles
80 g (2¾ oz) red cabbage, shredded

RED CABBAGE

SOBA NOODLES

EDAMAME

BARBECUED
CHICKEN

CARROT

CREAMY SESAME
DRESSING

TURKEY & WATERCRESS salad
WITH RANCH DRESSING

MAKES
1

RANCH DRESSING

2 tablespoons whole-egg mayonnaise
1 tablespoon buttermilk
2 teaspoons white-wine vinegar
½ garlic clove, crushed
1 tablespoon snipped chives
¼ teaspoon smoked paprika

Mix together.

OTHER INGREDIENTS

120 g (4½ oz) cooked turkey breast,
thinly sliced
1 celery stalk, thinly sliced
2 tablespoons dried cranberries
30 g (1 oz) toasted almonds
30 g (1 oz) parmesan cheese, shaved
1 large handful of watercress, to fill

WATERCRESS

PARMESAN CHEESE

TOASTED ALMONDS

DRIED
CRANBERRIES

CELERY

TURKEY

RANCH DRESSING

ITALIAN
CHICKEN SALAD

MAKES
1

RED-WINE VINAIGRETTE

2 tablespoons extra-virgin olive oil
1 tablespoon red-wine vinegar
½ teaspoon dijon mustard
salt & freshly ground black pepper

Mix together

ROASTED CAPSICUM

1 red capsicum (bell pepper)

**Roast in a 200°C (400°F) oven for
15–20 minutes, turning occasionally,
until the skin is charred and blistered.
Transfer to a sealable plastic bag and set
aside for 10 minutes to steam. Peel the skin
and discard. Remove and discard the stem
and seeds. Thickly slice.**

OTHER INGREDIENTS

50 g (1¾ oz) fresh mozzarella,
chopped into bite-sized pieces
120 g (4½ oz) barbecued chicken, shredded
2 tablespoons pine nuts
handful of roughly chopped basil
handful of rocket (arugula), to fill

ROCKET

BASIL

PINE NUTS

ROASTED CAPSICUM

BARBECUED
CHICKEN

RED-WINE
VINAIGRETTE

FRESH MOZZARELLA

CHICKEN
CAESAR SALAD

MAKES
1

CAESAR DRESSING

1 tablespoon whole-egg mayonnaise
1 tablespoon Greek-style yoghurt
squeeze of lemon juice
1 anchovy, finely chopped
1 small garlic clove, crushed
salt & freshly ground black pepper

Mix together.

CRISPY PROSCIUTTO

2 thin slices prosciutto

**Cook the prosciutto in a non-stick
frying pan over medium heat until golden.
Cool on paper towel, until crisp, then
roughly chop.**

GRILLED CHICKEN

100 g (3½ oz) chicken breast fillet,
cut into 2 cm (¾ inch) cubes
salt & freshly ground black pepper
olive oil, for frying

**Cook the chicken in a non-stick frying pan
over medium heat until golden. Remove
and allow to cool.**

CROUTONS

1 slice wholegrain bread (about 50 g/1¾ oz),
crusts removed, cut into 1 cm (½ inch) cubes
salt & freshly ground black pepper

**Arrange the cubes on a baking tray,
spray with oil and season. Toss to coat, bake
in a 200°C (400°F) oven for 6–8 minutes,
turning occasionally, until golden.**

OTHER INGREDIENTS

30 g (1 oz) parmesan cheese, shaved
handful of roughly chopped cos (romaine)
lettuce, to fill

COS LETTUCE

PARMESAN CHEESE

CROUTONS

CRISPY PROSCIUTTO

GRILLED CHICKEN

CAESAR DRESSING

CHICKEN & CABBAGE SALAD with ginger–miso DRESSING

MAKES
1

GINGER-MISO DRESSING

½ teaspoon sesame oil
3 teaspoons rice vinegar
1 teaspoon lemon juice
2 teaspoons white miso paste
½ teaspoon grated ginger
1 teaspoon caster (superfine) sugar

Mix together

OTHER INGREDIENTS

120 g (4½ oz) barbecued chicken, shredded
2 tablespoons toasted sesame seeds
50 g (1¾ oz) red cabbage, shredded
50 g (1¾ oz) white cabbage, shredded

WHITE CABBAGE

RED CABBAGE

TOASTED
SESAME SEEDS

BARBECUED
CHICKEN

GINGER-MISO
DRESSING

CONFIT DUCK
& BLOOD ORANGE SALAD

MAKES
1

BLOOD ORANGE VINAIGRETTE

2 tablespoons extra-virgin olive oil
2 tablespoons blood orange juice
½ teaspoon dijon mustard
salt & freshly ground black pepper

Mix together.

OTHER INGREDIENTS

1 blood orange, segments removed
and cut in half
1 cooked confit duck leg, flesh shredded
30 g (1 oz) toasted hazelnuts,
roughly chopped
handful of baby English spinach leaves, to fill

BABY SPINACH

TOASTED HAZELNUTS

BLOOD ORANGE
SEGMENTS

CONFIT DUCK

BLOOD ORANGE
VINAIGRETTE

CHICKEN, BEETROOT & WATERCRESS salad with roasted STRAWBERRY VINAIGRETTE

MAKES 1

ROASTED STRAWBERRY VINAIGRETTE

100 g (3½ oz) strawberries, hulled
1 tablespoon extra-virgin olive oil
1 tablespoon balsamic vinegar
½ teaspoon dijon mustard
salt & freshly ground black pepper

Roast the strawberries in a 220°C (430°F) oven for 15–20 minutes, until caramelised. Purée with other ingredients. Allow to cool.

ROASTED BEETROOT

1 beetroot (beet), unpeeled

Cover in foil and roast in a 180°C (350°F) oven for 45 minutes, or until a skewer can be inserted into the flesh. Allow to cool, pull off the skin, cut into 2 cm (¾ inch) pieces.

OTHER INGREDIENTS

120 g (4½ oz) barbecued chicken, shredded
1 small apple, cored and cubed
30 g (1 oz) walnuts
30 g (1 oz) feta, cubed
handful of watercress, to fill

WATERCRESS

FETA

WALNUTS

APPLE

BARBECUED
CHICKEN

ROASTED
BEETROOT

ROASTED STRAWBERRY
VINAIGRETTE

LEMON-POACHED
CHICKEN SALAD *with*
sorrel, sprouts & WALNUTS

MAKES
1

LEMON-MUSTARD DRESSING

2 tablespoons extra-virgin olive oil
1 tablespoon lemon juice
1 teaspoon dijon mustard
½ small garlic clove, minced
1 small French shallot, finely chopped
salt & freshly ground black pepper

Mix together.

OTHER INGREDIENTS

3 brussels sprouts, finely sliced
30 g (1 oz) toasted walnuts, roughly chopped
30 g (1 oz) parmesan cheese, finely grated
baby sorrel leaves, to fill

LEMON-POACHED CHICKEN

1 lemon, sliced
1 teaspoon whole black peppercorns
120 g (4½ oz) chicken breast fillet

Bring a small saucepan of water to the boil
with the lemon slices and peppercorns.
Reduce the heat, add chicken breast and
allow to simmer for 3 minutes (don't allow
it to come back to the boil). Remove
from the heat and let the chicken steep
in the poaching liquid for 10 minutes.
Remove from the pan and allow to
cool before shredding.

BABY SORREL

PARMESAN CHEESE

TOASTED WALNUTS

LEMON-POACHED
CHICKEN

BRUSSELS SPROUT

LEMON-MUSTARD
DRESSING

TURKEY
MEATBALL SALAD WITH
buttermilk dressing

MAKES
1

BUTTERMILK DRESSING

3 tablespoons buttermilk
juice of ½ lemon
1 tablespoon snipped chives
¼ teaspoon minced garlic
salt & freshly ground black pepper

Mix together.

TURKEY MEATBALLS

150 g (5½ oz) minced (ground) turkey
¼ small onion, finely chopped
2 teaspoons buttermilk
1 tablespoon snipped chives
½ small garlic clove, crushed
1 tablespoon finely grated parmesan
2 teaspoons Worcestershire sauce
4 drops Tabasco sauce
salt & freshly ground black pepper

**Mix together with hands until well
combined. Shape into walnut-sized balls.
Arrange on a baking tray and cook in a
200°C (400°F) oven for 20 minutes,
turning halfway through cooking.**

OTHER INGREDIENTS

1 carrot, peeled into strips
handful of cos (romaine) lettuce,
cut into bite-sized pieces

COS LETTUCE

TURKEY MEATBALLS

CARROT

BUTTERMILK
DRESSING

THAI
CHICKEN SALAD

MAKES
1

THAI CHICKEN

2 tablespoons salt-reduced chicken stock
120 g (4½ oz) chicken breast fillet,
finely chopped
3 teaspoons fish sauce
2 cm (¾ inch) piece of ginger,
finely chopped
½ long red chilli, seeded, finely chopped
½ teaspoon caster (superfine) sugar
2 teaspoons lime juice

Heat the stock in a frying pan over
medium–high heat, then add the chicken,
fish sauce and ginger. Cook, breaking up
the meat, for 5 minutes, or until browned
and cooked through. Add the chilli and
sugar and cook for 2 minutes. Transfer to
a bowl, stir through the lime juice
and set aside.

OTHER INGREDIENTS

30 g (1 oz) roasted peanuts, roughly chopped
1 Lebanese (short) cucumber,
cut in half, thinly sliced
handful each of coriander (cilantro),
mint & basil
handful of butter lettuce, cut into bite-sized
pieces, to fill
1 lime, cut into wedges

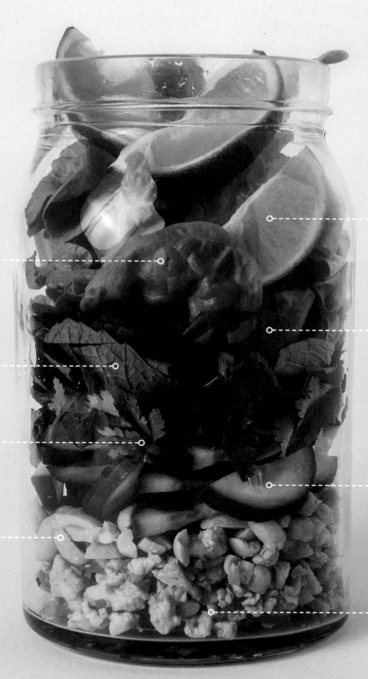

LIME WEDGES

BUTTER LETTUCE

BASIL

MINT

CORIANDER

CUCUMBER

ROASTED PEANUTS

THAI CHICKEN

Meat

BEEF TACO SALAD

MAKES
1

SALSA VINAIGRETTE

2 tablespoons extra-virgin olive oil
1 tablespoon lemon juice
1 tablespoon red-wine vinegar
2 tablespoons finely chopped jalapeños
100 g (3½ oz) cherry tomatoes, quartered
handful of finely chopped coriander (cilantro)

Mix together.

TACO SEASONING

1 teaspoon ground cumin
1 teaspoon freshly ground black pepper
½ teaspoon chilli powder
½ teaspoon salt
½ teaspoon smoked paprika
½ teaspoon garlic powder
½ teaspoon onion powder
½ teaspoon dried oregano

Mix together.

SEASONED BEEF

olive oil, for frying
½ small onion, finely chopped
Taco seasoning (recipe on right)
120 g (4½ oz) minced (ground) beef

Heat the oil in a frying pan over medium–high heat. Add the onion, and cook, stirring for about 3 minutes, until softened. Add the taco seasoning and cook, stirring, for about 30 seconds. Add the beef and cook, stirring, for 5–8 minutes, or until browned. Set aside to cool.

OTHER INGREDIENTS

½ avocado, diced, with lemon juice squeezed over
2 tablespoons shredded cheddar cheese
handful of cos (romaine) lettuce, cut into bite-sized pieces, to fill

COS LETTUCE

CHEDDAR CHEESE

SEASONED BEEF

AVOCADO

SALSA
VINAIGRETTE

PORK, FENNEL
& PINK LADY APPLE SALAD

MAKES
1

APPLE CIDER DRESSING

1 tablespoon extra-virgin olive oil
1 tablespoon apple-cider vinegar
½ teaspoon dijon mustard
salt & freshly ground black pepper

Mix together.

GRILLED PORK

150 g (5½ oz) pork fillet
salt & freshly ground black pepper
2 teaspoons olive oil

Season the pork and cook in the olive oil in an ovenproof char-grill pan over medium–high heat for a few minutes on each side, until seared. Transfer the pan to a 180°C (350°F) oven and cook for 10–12 minutes, until cooked through. Allow to rest before cutting into strips.

OTHER INGREDIENTS

¼ fennel bulb, finely sliced
1 pink lady apple, cored and cubed
handful of parsley, to fill

PARSLEY

PINK LADY APPLE

GRILLED PORK

FENNEL

APPLE CIDER
DRESSING

THAI BEEF
& HERB SALAD

MAKES
1

THAI DRESSING

1 teaspoon sesame oil
3 teaspoons lime juice
2 teaspoons fish sauce
½ teaspoon soy sauce
1 teaspoon finely grated ginger
1 small red chilli, seeded, finely chopped
2 teaspoons caster (superfine) sugar

Mix together.

GRILLED BEEF

150 g (5½ oz) piece beef fillet steak
salt & freshly ground black pepper
olive oil, for frying

**Season the steak and cook in the oil on
a char-grill pan for about 3 minutes each
side over high heat. Remove, allow to
cool, then thinly slice.**

OTHER INGREDIENTS

1 Lebanese (short) cucumber, diced
100 g (3½ oz) cherry tomatoes, halved
30 g (1 oz) roasted peanuts, roughly chopped
handful each of roughly chopped mint
& Thai basil

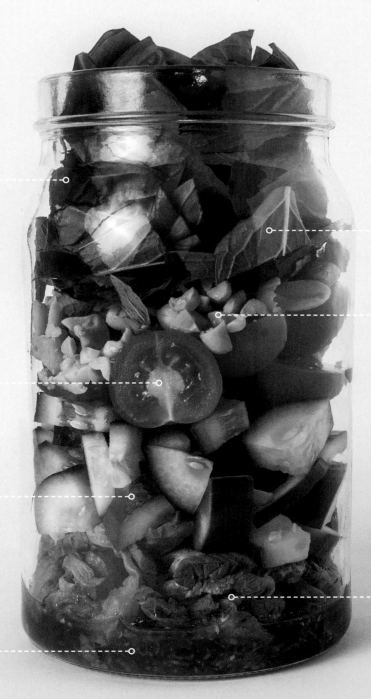

THAI BASIL

MINT

ROASTED PEANUTS

CHERRY TOMATO

CUCUMBER

GRILLED BEEF

THAI DRESSING

BROAD BEAN, PECORINO
& prosciutto salad

MAKES
1

LEMON VINAIGRETTE

2 tablespoons extra-virgin olive oil
1½ tablespoons lemon juice
½ teaspoon lemon zest
½ teaspoon dijon mustard
½ teaspoon caster (superfine) sugar
salt & freshly ground black pepper

Mix together.

BROAD BEANS

250 g (9 oz) frozen broad (fava) beans

**Blanch in boiling water for 3 minutes,
drop in ice water. Drain and remove skins.**

OTHER INGREDIENTS

4 slices prosciutto
50 g (1¾ oz) pecorino, roughly chopped
handful of roughly chopped mint
handful of baby sorrel leaves, to fill

BABY SORREL

MINT

PECORINO CHEESE

PROSCIUTTO

BROAD BEANS

LEMON
VINAIGRETTE

GREEK SALAD WITH
lamb MEATBALLS

MAKES
1

LEMON & OREGANO DRESSING

2 tablespoons extra-virgin olive oil
1 tablespoon lemon juice
2 teaspoons red-wine vinegar
½ teaspoon dried oregano
salt & freshly ground black pepper

Mix together.

LAMB MEATBALLS

120 g (4½ oz) minced (ground) lamb
½ onion, finely chopped
½ teaspoon dried oregano
½ lightly beaten egg
salt & freshly ground black pepper
2 teaspoons olive oil

**Combine the ingredients (apart from the oil)
and form into walnut-sized balls.
Arrange on a baking tray, drizzle with
the oil and cook in a 180°C (350°F) oven
for 15–20 minutes, turning halfway
through, or until cooked. Allow to cool.**

OTHER INGREDIENTS

1 Lebanese (short) cucumber, diced
100 g (3½ oz) cherry tomatoes, halved
50 g (1¾ oz) feta, cubed
handful of roughly chopped mint
cos (romaine) lettuce, chopped into
bite-sized pieces, to fill

COS LETTUCE

LAMB MEATBALLS

MINT

FETA

CHERRY TOMATO

CUCUMBER

LEMON & OREGANO
DRESSING

ROAST BEEF
& POTATO SALAD
with horseradish dressing

MAKES
1

HORSERADISH DRESSING

2 tablespoons extra-virgin olive oil
2 teaspoons red-wine vinegar
2 teaspoons horseradish cream
½ teaspoon dijon mustard

OTHER INGREDIENTS

3 small new potatoes, boiled,
cut into quarters
100 g (3½ oz) cherry tomatoes, halved
4 baby beetroot (beets), cut into quarters
120 g (4½ oz) roast beef slices
handful of watercress, to fill

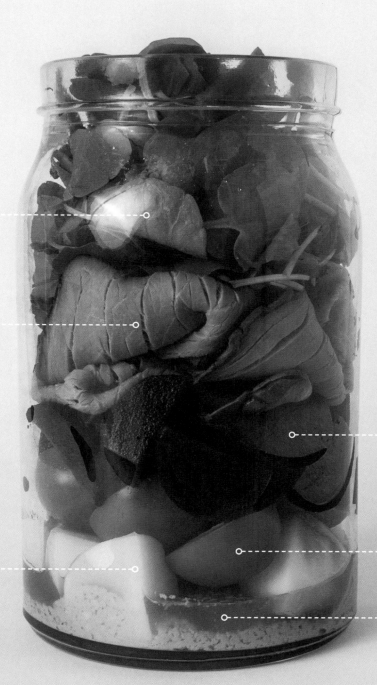

WATERCRESS

ROAST BEEF

BABY BEETROOT

NEW POTATO

CHERRY TOMATO

HORSERADISH
DRESSING

BARBECUED
HONEY & GINGER BEEF
with soba noodle salad

MAKES 1

LIME & SOY DRESSING

1 teaspoon sesame oil
1 tablespoon lime juice
1 teaspoon soy sauce

Mix together.

BARBECUED HONEY & GINGER BEEF

1 teaspoon honey
½ teaspoon grated ginger
120 g (4½ oz) beef rump or fillet steak
olive oil, for frying

Combine the honey and ginger and rub the mixture over the beef. Cook the steak on a char-grill pan over high for 3 minutes each side. Remove and set aside. Thinly slice.

OTHER INGREDIENTS

4 asparagus spears, sliced on a diagonal
1 small carrot, cut into matchsticks
100 g (3½ oz) cooked soba noodles
3 spring onions (scallions), thinly sliced
handful of coriander (cilantro), to fill

CORIANDER

BARBECUED HONEY
& GINGER BEEF

SPRING ONION

SOBA NOODLES

CARROT

ASPARAGUS

LIME & SOY
DRESSING

ROAST PUMPKIN, HALOUMI
& lamb salad

MAKES
1

POMEGRANATE DRESSING

2 tablespoons extra-virgin olive oil
juice of ½ lemon
2 teaspoons pomegranate molasses
salt & freshly ground black pepper

Mix together.

BARBECUED LAMB

150 g (5½ oz) lamb loin
salt & freshly ground black pepper
2 teaspoons olive oil

**Season the lamb and cook in the oil on
a char-grill pan over medium–high heat for
3–4 minutes on each side, or until cooked
to your liking. Allow to rest before slicing.**

ROASTED PUMPKIN

100 g (3½ oz) pumpkin (winter squash),
cut into 2 cm (¾ inch) pieces

Mix in a bowl with:

1 teaspoon olive oil
salt & freshly ground black pepper

**Once coated, tip onto a baking tray and
roast in a 180°C (350°F) oven for 15 minutes,
turning occasionally, or until cooked.
Allow to cool.**

GRILLED HALOUMI

2 teaspoons olive oil
50 g (1¾ oz) slice of haloumi

**Heat the oil in a frying pan over
medium–high heat, add the haloumi
and cook for 3 minutes on each side,
or until browned. Allow to cool,
cut into cubes.**

OTHER INGREDIENTS

handful of mixed salad leaves, to fill

MIXED
SALAD LEAVES

GRILLED HALOUMI

BARBECUED LAMB

ROASTED PUMPKIN

POMEGRANATE
DRESSING

VIETNAMESE GRILLED PORK, vermicelli & pickled VEGETABLE SALAD

MAKES 1

NUOC CHAM DRESSING

1 tablespoons white vinegar
3 teaspoons lime juice
2 tablespoons boiling water
1 tablespoons fish sauce
1 small red chilli, finely chopped
½ small garlic clove, crushed
3 teaspoons caster (superfine) sugar

Mix together until the sugar dissolves. Set aside to cool.

QUICK PICKLED VEGETABLES

125 ml (4 fl oz/½ cup) rice vinegar
3 tablespoons caster (superfine) sugar
1 teaspoon salt
½ carrot, cut into long matchsticks
½ Lebanese (short) cucumber, seeded, cut into long matchsticks

Mix the vinegar, sugar and salt until the sugar is dissolved. Add the carrot and cucumber. Cover and refrigerate for at least 1 hour before using.

GRILLED PORK

150 g (5½ oz) pork fillet
salt & freshly ground black pepper
2 teaspoons olive oil

Season the pork and cook in the olive oil in an ovenproof char-grill pan over medium–high heat for a few minutes on each side, until seared. Transfer the pan to a 180°C (350°F) oven and cook for 10–12 minutes, until cooked through. Allow to rest before cutting into 2 cm (¾ inch cubes).

OTHER INGREDIENTS

80 g (2¾ oz) cooked vermicelli noodles
handful each of coriander (cilantro) & mint

MINT

CORIANDER

PICKLED CUCUMBER

PICKLED CARROT

GRILLED PORK

VERMICELLI
NOODLES

NUOC CHAM
DRESSING

MIDDLE EASTERN BEEF SALAD

MAKES
1

TAHINI & SUMAC DRESSING

1 teaspoon extra-virgin olive oil
2 teaspoons lemon juice
2 tablespoons Greek-style yoghurt
1 tablespoon tahini
1 teaspoon sumac
salt & freshly ground black pepper
1–2 teaspoons water, to thin the dressing,
if necessary

Mix together.

SPICE MIX

1 teaspoon smoked paprika
1 teaspoon ground cumin
1 teaspoon ground coriander
1 teaspoon ground cinnamon
½ teaspoon salt
½ teaspoon freshly ground black pepper

Mix together.

SPICED BEEF

olive oil, for frying
½ onion, finely chopped
Spice mix (recipe on right)
150 g (5½ oz) minced (ground) beef
2 tablespoons pine nuts

Heat the oil in a frying pan over medium–high heat. Add the onion, and cook, stirring for about 3 minutes, until softened. Add the spice mix and cook, stirring, for about 30 seconds. Add the beef and pine nuts and cook, stirring, for 5–8 minutes, or until browned. Set aside to cool.

OTHER INGREDIENTS

1 Lebanese (short) cucumber, diced
30 g (1 oz) toasted cashews
handful each of roughly chopped parsley,
mint & coriander (cilantro)
handful of rocket (arugula), to fill

ROCKET

CORIANDER

MINT

PARSLEY

TOASTED CASHEWS

SPICED BEEF

CUCUMBER

TAHINI & SUMAC
DRESSING

INDEX

A

B

C

D

Published in 2016 by Smith Street Books
Melbourne | Australia
smithstreetbooks.com

ISBN: 978-1-925418-00-2

CIP data is available from the National Library of Australia

Publisher: Paul McNally
Design concept: Kate Barraclough
Design layout: Heather Menzies
Photographer: Hannah Koelmeyer
Photography assistants: Jo Briscoe, Aisling Coughlan,
    Michael Hart, Lucy Heaver, Lou Simpson & Jen Whyte

Printed & bound in China by C&C Offset Printing Co., Ltd.

Book 1
10 9 8 7 6 5 4 3 2 1